Louis Weber, CEO
Publications International, Ltd.
8140 Lehigh Avenue
Morton Grove, IL 60053

Images from Shutterstock.com

www.pilbooks.com

Manufactured in China.

8 7 6 5 4 3 2 1

ISBN: 978-1-64558-013-3

ANIMAL PUNS
NO PROB *llama*

new seasons®

I'm not fat . . . just a little husky.

Love is a four-legged word.

Egrets, I've had a few.

I could really gopher
some potato chips!

It's my first grey hare.

Whale, hello there!

Age is irr-elephant.

Do you think I should
switch to briefs?

Flying squirrel

Santa claws

Feeling philoslothical

Don't stop retrieving!

Wild goose chase.

I'm an animal of distinktion.

I'm in a fowl mood!

Owl be back.

I have friends in low places.

You think I'm tall?
Bet your giraffe I am!

I think I'm the cutest animal in the world.
I certainly have all the koalafications!

Ewe really need a haircut.

Beam me up, Scottie!

Lemur alone!

Frankly my dear, I don't give a dam.

Half ass

Kitty litter

Monkey see, monkey better not do.

Don't worry . . . bee happy!

Iguana go out for a walk.

You're no bunny 'til
some bunny loves you.

We may be pigs, but we are NOT boaring!

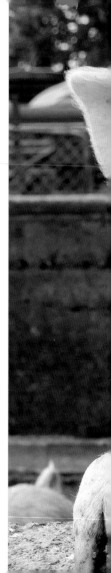

Wanna go on a picnic?
Alpaca lunch!

We're polar opposites.

He doesn't say much.
He's a little horse.

71

Toucan have more fun.

I hope I don't get a
ticket for littering.

That's pretty emusing!

Significant otters

Santa paws

You think I'm fat?
I think you're being
too hippo-critical.

That's the sealiest thing I've ever heard!

No prob-llama!

Crabs are SO shellfish!

You are my tweet-heart.

I can always spot a cheetah!

I love the World Wide Web.

Bone Appétit!

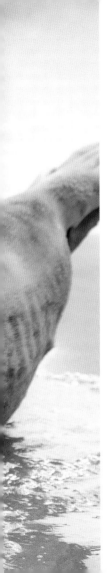

Slippery when wet.

You really quack me up!

100

Feline fine!

Easily a-moosed.

Mutts about you.

I can't bear to say goodbye.